DISCOURSES

BY

REV. SAMUEL T. SEELYE, D.D.,

AND

REV. CALVIN E. STOWE, D.D.,

DELIVERED AT

LOWELL, MASS., AND HARTFORD, CONN.,

BEFORE THE

SOCIETY FOR THE PROMOTION OF COLLEGIATE AND THEOLOGICAL EDUCATION AT THE WEST.

New-York:
JOHN A. GRAY & GREEN, PRINTERS AND STEREOTYPERS,
FIRE-PROOF BUILDINGS,
CORNER OF FRANKFORT AND JACOB STREETS.

1864.

gift
Tappan Presbyterian
6-4-45

DISCOURSE

BY

REV. SAMUEL T. SEELYE, D.D.*

"FOR the Lord giveth wisdom; out of his mouth cometh knowledge and understanding."—PROVERBS 2:6.

THIS passage of Scripture furnishes a theme that is especially appropriate to the present occasion. We learn from it that wisdom is a divine communication, and that knowledge is acquired by intercourse with God. It teaches us, not that education is important to Christianity, but that Christianity is essential to education.

Before entering upon the discussion of this subject, it may be well very briefly to show its relation to the Society for the Promotion of Collegiate and Theological Education at the West. That the aim of this Society is a noble one, is never questioned. All admit that the West must be supplied with colleges as well as with churches. It is, however, a question, whether the Church as such should plant and sustain them. Very many Christian men do not give an affirmative answer to this question. They hold that as the State builds hospitals and asylums, it should also found our colleges. What propriety, they ask, in pressing the claims of a Society like this upon Christians, and especially on the Sabbath? They regard the college as wholly a secular insti-

* "The thanks of the Board were presented to the Rev. Dr. Seelye for his discourse, delivered last evening, and a copy requested for publication." An extract from the Minutes of the Proceedings of the Directors of the Society for the Promotion of Collegiate and Theological Education at the West, at their Annual Meeting at Lowell, Mass., November 21st, 1860. JOHN SPAULDING, *Recording Secretary.*

tution. If the Church can bless it by her influence, and place Christian men at the head of it, so much the better. Just as it is better to have a Christian man at the head of an insane asylum than one who is not, if the latter be not more skillful than the former. If this position is correct, if the college can safely be left to the care of the State, or if the State without the aid of the Church can found and sustain the college, then this organization might as well be dispensed with at once. If, however, we can show that, like the preaching of the Gospel, it is so properly and specifically the work of the Church that it will not be done at all if she does not do it, then it will be admitted that this Society justly makes the strongest demand upon the sympathy and benevolence of every Christian heart. This will, we trust, be made apparent by the proof of our subject.

Whether education is considered as the acquirement of knowledge or as mental development, there can be none that deserves the name unless it be Christian.

1. Nothing of value can be taught concerning nature, if Christianity be not the teacher. Natural science will tell us of forces attractive and repellent, and of laws fixed and controlling. It will show us the strata of earth and rock which make up the world, and disclose the atoms which form the mass of every structure. It will reveal to us the original elements, and describe all the properties of matter. It will teach us the name of each plant and mineral, and make us familiar with all the varieties of shape and substance which are gathered in this treasury of creation. We may also learn, without the aid of Christianity, that the earth is a part of a system, which itself, with its sun and planets, forms but an insignificant part of the boundless universe. We may count the stars and measure their distances, and even weigh them in the balance. Yet is this knowledge? Do these forces and laws and properties really teach us any thing of nature? Neither the chemist, by the most careful analysis, nor the geologist, by the most patient investigation, can gain one true conception of nature, if the design of the Creator be not seen in his works. What progress has he made in mathematical science who can merely distinguish the numerals which it employs? How much does he know of language who has learned only the alphabet? Yet these material forms, of which alone mere natural sci-

ence can tell us any thing, are but the letters of a language. Of themselves alone they are worthless. It is only when grouped together into words that they can embody thoughts, and teach us truths. All acquaintance with nature that does not go beyond the mere phenomena which she presents, is as fruitless as the mere knowledge of the alphabet of a foreign language. What knowledge could be gained of the master-piece of Raphael, by overlooking the grand conception of the artist in a most careful analysis of the colors and the canvas? He who thus studies nature, as he sums up his worthless attainments, may well cry out in despair: "Where shall wisdom be found, and where is the place of understanding? The depth saith, It is not in me; and the sea saith, It is not with me."

Yet with Christianity as a teacher, these material forms tell us of something more than properties and laws. She shows us the Creator in his works, and thrills our soul by the great truth that "in the beginning God created the heaven and the earth." Nature is no longer a meaningless combination of atoms and elements. It is an exhibition of Divine skill and Infinite goodness. Its laws are expressions of the Divine will, and all its varied phenomena show something of the plan and the attributes of its Author. "The sea is his, and he made it: and his hands formed the dry land. By his knowledge the depths are broken up, and the clouds drop down the dew. His covenant is with day and night, and he hath appointed the ordinances of heaven and earth. The heavens declare his glory, and the firmament showeth his handiwork." With Christianity as our teacher, the study of nature is no longer limited to the mere properties of matter; but every law and force and form, tell us something of God. Can there be any knowledge of nature with God left out of view?

2. Our knowledge of history is worthless, except as Christianity interprets the events of the past. We might indeed without her aid know the bare facts of history. But how meaningless would be the record! We might learn the struggles, the achievements, and the defeats of each successive generation. Yet what bond would unite them together? what truth would they teach if they did not exhibit a Divine purpose and plan? The events of the past are perverted, and made to teach that which is false, if God be not seen in them all. If history tells us only of disap-

pointed hopes, and the vain strife of human passion; if it teaches us only what the skill of man has accomplished; if it narrates only the rise and growth and decay of governments, it proclaims a stupendous falsehood. For the events of the past were not designed to show us the value of forms of government, nor to teach us the limits of human power, but to reveal the eternal sovereignty, the inflexible justice and infinite love of God. From the fall of man to the birth of Christ the centuries were employed in preparing for his coming; and from the crucifixion to the present moment, they have been preparing for his triumph. The student of history, therefore, who fails to grasp these truths is engaged in a fruitless task. He can only be deceived.

What could he know of machinery who should see only the shuttle as it flashes across the loom? If he looks no further what must be his impressions? He must believe that the shuttle is animated by a power of its own, and for a purpose of its own. Yet all the while, far down below, the great wheel is steadily revolving, sending through many an agent its own impulse to the shuttle. Of this, the real moving power, he could learn nothing. So he who studies history without going back to the sovereign power which shapes and marshals its events, must believe that which is false. "History," says a German philosopher, "is the inspired gift of God, employing itself to illuminate the dark ways of God." A still better definition is that of Bolingbroke, as amended by one of the ablest of our American scholars. He defines history to be "God teaching by examples." With either definition we see that the mere record of past events which does not recognize God is not history. He must be seen in it all, unfolding his own plan, and accomplishing his own purpose in each event, or there can be no knowledge of the past.

Again, it can also be easily shown that all conceivable attainments, all that men call knowledge, must be rejected as unsatisfying if God be shut out. The soul can not rest till it has overleaped every bound, and attained the infinite. Neither the intellect nor the will, nor the heart, can be at rest without God. The intellect finds that there is a limit to its knowledge till it knows God. The will is conscious of misdirected and wasted energy till it moves in harmony with the will of God. The heart feels that all the wealth of its love is thrown away upon an idol till it is given to God. Man, with all his insignificance, yea, because of his insignificance, rejects every thing as unsatisfying till he lays hold on God. Yet the knowledge of God does not satisfy unless it be of God in Christ. In order to approach him, and be able to cry, Abba, Father, these sins which separate us from him must be taken away. We hear only the stern demands of justice, and see only the terrible penalty of a broken law, till God appears incarnate, and with the power and willingness to pardon, says with infinite tenderness: "Come unto me." In him, and in him alone, can the soul find rest. Of what value is all other knowledge in comparison with this? What truth has he gained that is worth possessing, who knows nothing of God manifest in the flesh—the Saviour of the world? Is not Christianity, therefore, which evermore points us to this Saviour, the only teacher that is qualified for the office?

3. Education, regarded as mental development, can not be adequately secured without the aid of Christianity. The mind grows by the acquirement of knowledge. The expansion of its powers is determined by the truth which it is able to grasp. For its highest development, therefore, it needs the highest kind of truths. Yet we have seen that its unaided efforts to gather truth, either from nature or the past, are alike in vain. It can only be baffled and deceived. Christianity must create for it a true science and a correct philosophy, and give it a history to study. Any proper mental development is therefore impossible, except under the influence of Christianity. Those truths, however, which it is the peculiar province of Christianity to unfold, are essential to the fullest developments, because they are the highest of all truths. For they pertain to the character and attributes of God, and the eternal destiny of the soul. All other truths are petty and worthless in comparison with these.

A few years before his death, Daniel Webster, at a dinner-party in New-York, sat for a long time silent and abstracted. Repeated attempts were made to arouse him, but in vain. Finally, one of the gentlemen present asked him what was the greatest thought that ever entered his mind? His eye kindled in a moment, and he replied: "The greatest thought that ever entered my mind is the thought of God, and my relation to him." Surely no greater thought than that ever entered any mind. To conceive of God as Christianity reveals him, and to learn the plans of his mercy toward us, is to grasp the sublimest of truths. That mind must remain forever dwarfed which has no such conception of God.

There is, however, an essential requisite to the highest mental development, which should not be overlooked. The spiritual must be emancipated from its bondage to the animal. Unless reason becomes supreme over sense, every effort at mental development will only make its bondage more degrading. Yet what can overturn the sovereignty of the sense, and make reason supreme? What can bring the cravings of the animal into unquestioning submission to the behests of the spiritual? Human philosophy here confesses her impotence. The work is far beyond her power. If man becomes conscious of his degradation, that consciousness can only drive him to despair. For in all the universe there is no power that can work out his deliverance. Every system of education devised by human wisdom can only confirm the supremacy of the animal nature. On this account, the triumphs of civilization, and the utmost refinement of art, can confer no lasting blessings. They can never give to man that which he most needs—liberty. All their influence renders the enslavement of the spiritual more complete. Christianity alone, so much as promises freedom. She alone even tries to arouse the conscience, by whose decision the crown must be placed upon the reason. She arrays before it the great principles of eternal right, and demands for them its support. Conscience responds to the demand, and for the first time the spiritual has hope of triumph.

Yet with this victory of the spiritual, the work of education is not finished. The full stature of perfection can be attained only in Christ Jesus. The man is not complete till his manhood is glorified by Christian faith. He can be fitted for great achievements only through its power, and his heart swells with satisfying joy only as that hope which is the offspring of this faith becomes an anchor to his soul. By faith he is united to God, and the glory of the Highest is his eternal crown. The province of gospel faith is higher than that of human reason, as the reason is above the sense. Christianity alone raises the soul up to this higher and wider domain. She places the sense in just subjection to the reason, and brings the reason under the still higher power of Gospel faith. Under her teachings, the mind grows by the acquirement of knowledge; the spiritual nature rejoices in its freedom, and the soul is fitted to attain the highest destiny. This is the glorious fruit of Christian education. Compare it with the results which all other systems have attained, and you will be persuaded that no other true education is possible.

This leads me to say that these conclusions of our reason are fully affirmed by history. It declares that there never has been any true and adequate education except through Christianity. There has been great progress in art without her aid. Yet the mind has always been deluded by falsehood; that knowledge which alone can satisfy has never been attained, and the most sublime of all truths have not developed the powers of the intellect. Aside from this, moreover, the idea of attaining a nobler manhood for its own worth was never conceived; nor has there ever been so much as an attempted deliverance from the bondage of sense, except under the influence of Christianity. The old philosophies were intended to give greater refinement to sensual indulgence, and even this seeming blessing was to be conferred only on the favored few. The idea that man as man, is of worth and has rights, has never been conceived except as Christianity has taught it. To the cultivated few, the masses were always the vulgar herd, the ignorant rabble, unworthy the efforts of those more highly favored. For their improvement no philosopher ever toiled, and human learning denied them even the crumbs which fell from its table. Even the right of man to civil liberty was never declared till Christianity proclaimed it. In the Athenian Republics the idea of freedom for man as man was never developed. The blessings of liberty were to be given only to the free-born citizens of the Republic. Plato, in his ideal of a model state, gained no such conception of the rights of man. The man was merged and lost in the State. Neither Socrates nor Aristotle, nor any other moralist or philosopher, untaught by the Bible, ever grasped the great truth, that man, in whatever clime he dwells, has a God-given right to be free. The development of this sublime truth was reserved for Christianity alone. Save under her influence, no right has ever been conceded to the mass of the people, and there has been no thought of improving their condition. No system of false religion, no kind or degree of civilization, and no form of government have ever been able to free the masses from oppression and ignorance. Such has always been the structure of society, where the influence of the Gospel has not formed it, that a plan of universal education would necessitate a revolution. Christianity alone seeks to distribute to all with impartial hand the choicest blessings. She asserts the infinite worth of every human soul. She sends her servants into the highways and hedges, to invite the outcast and the degraded to her richest feast. She bestows her priceless gifts upon the lowest as well as the highest. The poor fisherman, the dishonest publican, and the degraded Magdalen, are offered the same blessings as the rich and the honored. Jesus Christ himself taught the multitude, and preached the Gospel to the poor. It is for this reason that Christianity has provided the means of education for the masses, and that universal education is possible under her influence alone. The Church of Christ has proved herself to be the light of the world, because she has been the only educator of the world. From no other source has the light of learning ever been shed abroad, diffusing its blessings to every class. Our fathers were led to plant colleges, not as politicians, but as Christians; not for the sake of the State, but for the sake of the Church. A college whose doors are open to all is a Christian institution; its very plan shows the influence of the Gospel. These Eastern colleges have grown strong and vigorous, because they were founded and have been nurtured by Christian men. The Church planted them as a part of her great work in the strict fulfillment of her mission. If the East had been settled by godless men, these colleges, which are now her glory and her strength, would never have been established. Look over the land to-day and see the proof of this truth. Wherever the Christian element prevails, there only is the college really demanded, and there only can it be sustained. We need not go beyond our own borders to learn that the power to educate is in the Church, and that the cause of education prospers just in proportion to the strength of the Church. The state with all its resources can not make a college. Neither the pride nor the pecuniary interests of peculiar localities can build up a college. The Christian element in the character of the people must lay its corner-stone, and rear its walls, and provide its endowment. It may be aided by the patriot and philanthropist, and receive contributions even from pride and selfish interest. Just as in building churches, and in sending missionaries to the heathen, the ungodly may lend a helping hand; yet, after all, the work is the work of the Church. If, moreover, this work be neglected, Christianity herself must suffer. It is as essential to her own life that she should found the college as that she should rear the family altar and the sanctuary. We are asked to sustain colleges at the West for precisely the same reason that we are asked to build churches and send missionaries there. The Christian element is already there demanding the college for education as truly as the Church for worship. Prevent its complete development by withholding the college, and you will crush out that element as truly as by withholding the Church. For the college is not a luxury which can be dispensed with, but a necessity. It is necessary not only to the glory of the State, but to the prosperity of the Church. If we refuse to plant colleges at the West, no other effort put forth in its behalf can accomplish any permanent good.

This Society, therefore, makes the strongest possible appeal to Christians at the East. It asks us to nurture the colleges at the West, which have been already founded by those who learned at the East, or from the East, that education must be Christian. It appeals to Christian men to do a Christian work, and it makes its appeals for the sake of Christ and the Church. It asks us to make permanent the influence of the Gospel, by endowing the most permanent of all Christian institutions.

No other Society seeks a nobler object, or possesses stronger claims upon the sympathy and cordial support of the disciples of Christ.

DISCOURSE

BY

REV. CALVIN E. STOWE, D.D.*

THE WORD OF GOD APPLIED BY THE SPIRIT OF GOD THE SOVEREIGN REMEDY FOR THE MISERIES OF MEN.

"SEEING ye have purified your souls in obeying the truth through the Spirit unto unfeigned love of the brethren, see that ye love one another with a pure heart fervently: Being born again, not of corruptible seed, but of incorruptible, by the word of God, which liveth and abideth forever. For all flesh is as grass, and all the glory of man as the flower of grass. The grass withereth, and the flower thereof falleth away. But the word of the Lord endureth forever. And this is the word which by the gospel is preached unto you."—1 PETER 1: 22–25.

OUR text teaches that, selfish and corrupt as men are, they can be brought to disinterested love and entire purity, when born again of incorruptible seed, by means of the word of God. That *seed* and *word* here do not mean the same thing is evident from the change of prepositions, εκ before σπορας, denoting the efficient cause, and δια before λογου the instrument or means. That the *word* (λογος) is the spoken and written revelation, and not the personal Logos, is evident from the last verse, where it is interchanged with ρημα, *and this is the word* (ρημα) *which by the Gospel is preached unto you.*

In order to love and purity, then, according to our text, men must be born again, not of the old and corruptible seed of nature,

* The thanks of the Board were presented to Rev. Dr. Stowe for his Sermon preached last evening, and a copy requested for publication." —An extract from the Minutes of the Proceedings of the Directors of the Society for the Promotion of Collegiate and Theological Education at the West, at their annual meeting at Hartford, Ct., November 11, 1863. JOHN SPAULDING, Recording Secretary.

which gives their first and sinful birth, but born again of the new and incorruptible seed of the Spirit, proceeding directly from God, and made to germinate by means of that word of God, proclaimed in the Gospel, which liveth and abideth forever, while all human things fade away.

No one, as it seems to me, can look upon men as they now exist, and as they always have existed in all ages of their history, without seeing the necessity of their being regenerated, born again, if they would at all become the worthy offspring of a God of love and purity. When I look at the human race just as it is, and just as it always has been from the earliest period of its history, I am astonished at the superficial views of those who affirm that human nature is not depraved, and that men need only cultivate and train and educate what they have by nature, and that thus they can become good and perfect without regeneration or the supernatural workings of God's Spirit in the soul; and I am equally amazed at the presumption of those philosophers and theologians, who undertake to account satisfactorily for the existence of man just as he is, and to show clearly how it is that such a creation, in its present condition, is an honor to God and a good to the universe. When I read these theories, propounded usually with such an air of self-complacency, it seems to me, if the authors are really sincere in their assumptions, it must be that they have never seen the actual condition of mankind, and know but little of the nature and character of men as they really are.

Precisely why God has made just such a world as this, and put into it just such a race, in just such a condition, as has always occupied it, I believe nobody knows; and all professedly rational and satisfactory accounts of the matter, which have ever yet been given, are, as I see them, but a mockery to the earnest, a foolery to the thoughtful, and a sham to all mankind. And this entirely apart from all theories of the origin of sin, or of the corruption of our nature; and taking only the facts which lie upon the very surface of the history of man. For His own glory and the highest good of the universe, no doubt; but how? in what way? why precisely by this process rather than by some other involving less of sin and shame and agony? why was not some other way possible? These are questions which we are constantly asking, and to which we never get a satisfactory answer. And if we can not get satisfactory answers to these questions, it matters very little whether other subordinate speculative questions are answered or not. It is all an inexplicable mystery, and we can only say: "*Even so, Father, for so it seemed good in thy sight.*" God knows if we do not, and he has given proof of his love in the gift of his Son for our salvation.

Look at men as a whole just as they are now, and just as they always have been ever since they began to exist. I do not say this or that exceptional individual, or this or that exceptional community; but all men of all ages and all regions, and all races, by whom the world has ever been peopled, and is now peopled, and considering each individual of this countless multitude as an immortal soul, capable of bearing the image of God intellectually and ethically, and expanding through all eternity in the divine glories of mental greatness and moral goodness, and is not the actual condition of the human race a mystery?

Observe the lower stratum of population in all great cities, from the beginning of the world to the present time. Millions on millions of individuals, each an immortal soul, capable of the highest development, living and dying like the brutes that perish, without even the physical comforts and advantages which the brutes themselves have, and that, too, in the midst of the most Christian nations. What does God want of so many human creatures of such sorts? Why not have fewer and of better quality? Who knows? How many thousands, nay millions, of Australians, and Feejees, and Diaks, and of whatever savage names, have lived and died, are still living and dying, on this earth, apparently never rising in the scale of being perceptibly above the rank of rats and reptiles! And are these God's immortal souls, created in his image and destined to his eternity? Will you explain it to me how and why it is? Or go to equatorial Africa, the land of the monstrous gorilla, and show me God's offspring there, in the human inhabitants, whose most relishing and delicious food is the gigantic monkey, the boa constrictor, and each other—a kind of food which certainly has the advantage of great economy and abundant reproductiveness. Can you make the reason, the final cause of this, all plain to the understanding? Yet these horrible savages, disgusting and loathsome as they seem to us, are morally no worse than, possibly not so bad as, the many of the classically cultivated and wonderfully intellectual Greeks and Romans, as they are described to us by their own historians, Thucydides, and Tacitus, and Suetonius, and by the Apostles in the New Testament.

Indeed it seems to me that the capabilities of the human race for wickedness and degradation have never yet been fully described or even adequately conceived by the most terrible of the theological writers on total depravity; and on the other hand the capacity for elevation and refinement is equally wonderful. These human creatures, all and each, collectively and individually, are God's offspring, immortal souls, capable of regeneration and eternal life. They can, each one of them, be born again of incorruptible seed, by means of the word of God, and brought to love and purity and an eternity of spiritual, God-like life. We have the experimental proof of actual fact that many of the most degraded and most wicked of the human race have been, by the spirit and word of God, made pure and noble and good, evidencing the possibility of such a regeneration.

Besides this extreme and gross though by no means exaggerated view of what that human nature is which is to be regenerated and sanctified by the spirit of God through the means of his word, let us take a nearer and more interior look at the actual fact as it exists among the most cultivated nations, where the Gospel for ages has been the civilizer, and where all the institutions of the Christian religion are found in full operation. Without at all ignoring, but with full and grateful recognition of the fact of a great amount of individual excellence and social purity and happiness in Christian nations, yet even in them the deplorable effects of depravity are but too plainly seen.

1. Sins of the spirit by the perversion of the natural susceptibilities.

Avarice. A prudent foresight of future needs perverted to a mere love of acquisition, saying to the gold, Thou art my hope, and to the most fine gold, Thou art my confidence, whence extortion and all its miseries, slavery and all its demoralizations, and infinite suffering among men.

Ambition. A laudable desire to excel perverted to a towering determination to trample others under foot at whatever expense of treasure and blood. Hence desolating wars, destruction, devastation and wretchedness.

Envy. Where one can neither acquire nor excel, the indulgence of a morbid hatred toward those who can; the meanest of all mean passions, yet one of the most common, even among Christians and clergymen.

2. Sins of the flesh by the perversion of the natural appetites.

Gluttony. The natural and necessary relish for food perverted to an indulgence worse than brutal, for brutes seldom over-eat.

Drunkenness. The necessary desire for drink perverted to an indulgence which brings misery unspeakable, every day and every moment, upon a very large portion of the human race, and brutalizes the human soul.

Lust. The relation between the sexes which God has chosen as the most fitting symbol of the relation between himself and the devout soul, the foundation of some of the purest and most ecstatic joys of life. Oh! the untold miseries arising from its perversion in all ages and nations, and in every Christian as well as in every pagan community.

And withal, the almost universal stupidity and recklessness in regard to sin; and all these perversions and horrors the most common and every-day occurrences, in all ages, in all nations, in the most Christian lands, from the beginning of history to the present day.

And religion, the Christian religion inself, intended by God as the cure of all these evils, by a most wonderful ingenuity of depravity, instead of diminishing, is often made to aggravate them all, through ethical errors and fearful superstitions, through the narrowness of bigotry and the ferocious cruelty of persecution.

And this remedial religion has never been put in the possession of a tenth part of the human race, who all are to be saved by it, or they have no method of salvation revealed to us. No wonder the best Christians sometimes groan in mental and bodily agony, and are almost ready to sink to hopeless despair, especially when they place the actual facts side by side with the miserable, futile, abortive attempts of philosophers and theologians to account for them and give a rational vindication of them. So the seaman sometimes, in a dark and tempestuous night, out of his reckoning and with only the uncertain glimmer of a distant lighthouse to guide him, must just put head to the wind, hold hard on the helm, and wait for the subsiding of the storm and the rising of the daylight. Better in such cases no chart at all than a chart constructed in ignorance of the soundings of the deep and the bearings of the coast.

Perhaps in all the developments of human depravity and blindness and weakness, there is nothing more discouraging and painful than the misuse of the remedies which men propose and apply for the alleviation and cure of the evils under which they suffer.

The science of politics and the art of government are perverted to tyranny and oppression, to war and anarchy, and nearly one half of the miseries of the world have arisen from the conflicts between the governments and the peoples. And what can excite a more intense indignation than a history of the opinions and feelings and actions of the governing classes generally in all generations in respect to the governed?

Physicians, sometimes, with the most benevolent intentions adopt theories in regard to disease and apply medicines which torture instead of alleviating, and exasperate instead of curing—and after there is good reason to suspect all is not right, there are some who still go on with the most wiry pertinacity, and in blind adherence to their theory torment and kill for the benefit of science as conscientiously as persecuting inquisitors for the good of the Church and the glory of God.

The theologian, too, in his anxiety to vindicate the ways of God to men, and thus reconcile men to God, often makes ten puzzles in solving one, inspires hate where he would induce love, and destroys the soul instead of saving it. And yet he perseveres, for he is sure his explanations ought to be satisfactory, and if they do harm rather than good, it is because men are depraved, and not because he has undertaken to tell more than he knows.

For universal obligatory belief, for the salvation of the soul and the conversion of the world, the simple, direct, aphoristic, matter-of-fact teachings of the Bible are enough without the jointings and tinkerings and inharmonious harmonizings of speculative philosophy. It is the sincere milk of the word which men need in order that they may grow thereby; and not the hard, biting, indigestible cheese which theologians so often make of it. Not that theologians are blameworthy for speculating; it is the nature of mind to investigate and to systematize. As Lord Bacon truly says: "The human understanding is active, and can not halt or rest, but, even though without effect, still presses forward." The fault is not in the speculating, that is all right and useful when kept in its proper sphere. The fault is in imposing the results of these speculations upon others, as articles of faith, and insisting upon it that these theories shall relieve the difficulties of others, because perhaps they may have relieved our own, when their only effect is and must be in certain minds to disturb and destroy. The doctrine itself is difficult enough, but the explanation is a hundred-fold more so. The real facts of theology are hard enough, but the theories invented to ease and smooth over the facts are ten times harder than the facts themselves. Says the philosopher to the troubled inquirer: "The pill, I know, is a bitter one, it needs a little coating; come, I will put it into this chestnut burr, and then you will not taste the bitter as it goes down. Now gape, sinner, and swallow, and be thankful for a Meg Merrilies who can make hard things easy to you."

Thus the effect of the word is hindered by many who desire to be its promoters; the injudicious defenses of its friends are more fatal to its success than the fiercest assault of its foes; and men are driven into sin and darkness by those who really wish to lead them into the light of the Lord.

The condition of the human race, physically and morally, is a dark mystery to us all, and there is no sufficient explanation of it; but one thing we do know, and that is a satisfaction, even if we know nothing else—God has put into our hands a remedy for the moral ills of man, and ultimately for the physical—a remedy unchangeable, infallible, always effective—his word—and this remedy we can always apply with a certainty of success.

Attend again to the declarations of the Apostle: "Seeing ye have purified your souls in obeying the truth through the spirit unto unfeigned love of the brethren, see that ye love one another with a pure heart fervently: Being born again, not of corruptible seed, but of incorruptible, by the word of God, which liveth and abideth forever. For all flesh is grass, and all the glory of man as the flower of grass. The grass withereth and the flower thereof falleth away: But the word of the Lord endureth forever. And this is the word which by the gospel is preached unto you."

The effect of this word is to produce sincerity and love, not hypocrisy and hate. It is the truth of God operating by the efficiency of the Spirit of God. Here is something for us to busy ourselves with—here is scope enough for all the activity of our nature—and here our powers can always be usefully employed.

Sickening and distressing as is the view of men in their depravity and debasement, yet the human creature is, after all, the noblest of God's works which ever meet our eye, especially when this degenerate creature is born again, not of the corruptible seed, but of the incorruptible, by means of the word of God, which liveth and abideth forever. What more lovely, more delightful, more perfectly admirable, than the cultivated, regenerated, sanctified Christian man or woman, than the thoroughly Christianized community of men? Yet these men are the brethren of all other men, and it is God's Spirit and God's word which raises them above the common level of the race. And the word acts by no magic energy. It is the ideas and principles of the word, transfused into the soul by aid of the Spirit's power, which produces the effect.

But to prevent mutilations, corruptions, and perversions, it is necessary that this word be committed to writing, fixed and permanent on the alphabetic page. The book is better than the Church (that keeps the book indeed but hides it) as the depository of divine truth. That portion of nominal Christendom (and it is much the largest portion numerically) which makes church tradition superior to or coördinate with the written revelation, and has withheld the Bible from the people, has smothered the divine truth under a mass of the commandments of men. From the earliest times they have chosen the ship as the emblem of the Church; and with them the old bottom has become so encumbered with an aggregation of traditionary barnacles, that she can scarcely move, she barely floats and drifts, and makes no progress. But on the book, open to the eyes of all, and with freedom of thought and discussion, there can be no permanent aggregation of barnacles. The ship is hauled into dock at very frequent intervals, and where freedom prevails, every man is at hand with his scraper to keep the bottom clear and smooth; and the old ship of the true spiritual Church of Christ is so solidly built that it will endure any amount of scraping without injury. The word is stable; there it stands from age to age; and whatever changes may take place in opinions, in philosophy, in institutions, in social life, there is the old text, just as it always was, just as it always will be. There may be misunderstandings, there may be perverse interpretations, there may be dogmatic glosses; but while the text remains, the inevitable result of thorough investigation will be to wheel men round at last to the true meaning of the word again. The ship may turn with the tide and veer with the wind; but while the mooring holds, she can never break quite away nor go entirely adrift; and she will certainly bring round right when the wind goes down and the tide finds its level. While there is a written word, intelligible, unequivocal, error must be temporary and mutable, not permanent nor steadily progressive.

To us, in regard to spiritual and eternal things, there is an absolute necessity for a reliable book, an objective revelation, sure and infallible. The late Theodore Parker once told me that he no more felt the need of an infallible revelation on religion than on chemistry. It struck me that there were some very essential differences in the two cases. Chemistry lies entirely within the bounds of natural knowledge, religion does not. We can detect the mistakes of chemists by our own investigations in the world of nature, as open to us as to the chemist, but who can go into the spirit lands, and there detect the mistakes of the religious philosophers, and come back and let us know? By the time the mistake is ascertained it is too late to correct it. Moreover, chemistry pertains only to material things and this short life; but religion to spiritual things, which fix our destinies for eternity. I must have an infallible, objective revelation on religion, or I must discard religious thought altogether, and live wholly in and for the world of sense.

This divine word, however, this regenerating word on which so much depends, to us and to all mankind, at the present day, (and so it will continue to the end of time,) is locked up in ancient and foreign languages, formed under strange and unknown climes and customs, to be perfectly learned only by hard and long continued study, with ample literary apparatus; and a kind of study, too, which to most men, as I have had ample opportunity to know by forty years' experience in teaching, is extreme weariness to the flesh. Yet here is the only avenue to this divine word; for there are no Scriptures plenarily inspired but the original Scriptures, and the gift of tongues has ceased. God has deposited his word among us in this way. This is God's method for man's access to it, and woeful defeat awaits any organized body of God's army who neglect to come to his arsenal, by this the only gate which he has opened.

The pure and effective application then of this, the only infallible remedy which God has provided for the sins and woes of mankind, requires, in every community, the establishment of colleges and literary institutions of the highest order. This has always been known and acknowledged in every Christian nation. Not one man in a hundred, no, not one in a thousand, of all who go into the ministry, ever have the taste, zeal, and energy to pursue this study effectively in private; and even where this thousandth man is found, he can not, from his individual resources, collect a competent literary apparatus for the purpose. Nor is the individual mind, without the help and collision of other associated minds, able to make a clear passage through the thorny paths of ancient linguistic study.

Nor the ancient languages alone, but also the modern. The varied forms of human thought, to as wide an extent as possible, should be called in to the aid of him, who would ascertain clearly the meaning of God's word for himself, and learn how effectively and fully to communicate that meaning to others. Not that every minister must be an accomplished linguist himself; but he must learn how to breathe in an atmosphere of linguistic learning, and be able to avail himself of the acquisitions of others.

And not languages only, but the sciences, all, must contribute their quota to the art of divine interpretation; for all truth is from God, natural as well as spiritual—Creation and the Bible are both from him, and all truth is homogeneous, harmonious, self-consistent. If, then, any supposed truths of natural science and of revelation seem to conflict with each other, we are precisely in the condition of the arithmetician, who has done his sum, as he thinks correctly, but finds that it will not prove; he must go all over it again, both the sum and the proof, and detect the hidden mistake; for he knows, by the result, that there must be a mistake somewhere.

Want of harmony shows there is error, and there is no real conflict anywhere between a truth of natural science and a truth of theology; and an apparent conflict only shows the need of a re-investigation, either in our science or in our theology, and probably in both. And how is this to be accomplished without institutions of learning of the highest order? The institutions must be fitted to the communities in which they exist. They must begin small where the communities are small, and grow proportionately, keeping pace with society around them.

I know institutions may be perverted, but so far as the interpretation of the Bible is concerned, if they are really learned institutions, they can not long be perverted; for real learning, applied to the Bible, inevitably leads to an understanding of what its teachings really are, and not all the dogmatic prejudice, or scientific scorn, or sectarian blindness in the world can effectually prevent or long retard this result.

Let no one say we must have the meeting-houses first and the colleges afterwards. We must have them both together.

In the old church, the chief meeting-house in a district was always also the college for the education of its ministers.

This practice, we are told by the ancient fathers, was introduced by the Apostle John, who established a school of this kind in the principal church at Ephesus.

Supposing men should say, let us have the paddle-wheels, for our steamboats—the paddle-wheels, by all means—we can get them cheap, we can make them ourselves with a little help; but as to the engines, they are cumbrous, complicated, expensive things. The material must be brought from a distance; the best of workmen must be employed at high wages; we will wait till we are richer before we get them. I know it is possible to work the paddle-wheels, if they are very small ones, by hand or by horse-power, but not long or to much advantage. We must have the engines, or the paddle-wheels will do but little.

And if you are poor, you will be a long while growing rich enough without your engines to enable you to get them. You must have your engines before you can get your start out of your poverty. Your boats will do nothing effectively without both engines and paddle-wheels, and you must have them both to begin with.

By the appointment of Christ himself, and as the necessities of the case most obviously require, a class of men are set apart from all other employments to devote themselves to the study of God's word, that they may be its interpreters to the people.

These men know that they have no miraculous gifts, either of inspiration or of tongues, and that their qualifications must be the result of their own industry and fidelity in the use of the opportunities which God has given them. Dare such men assume to be interpreters of God's word, without being able to read it themselves, as God gives it to them? Dare they take this responsible office, without doing all in their power to make themselves as ready as possible in the original languages of the Holy Scriptures?

Not that every minister is bound to be an accomplished linguist; but every minister who can do it, is bound to make the original Scriptures his ultimate appeal both for doctrine and practice; and to take the words of God as God originally uttered them, and make these words the basis of his instructions to the people.

But perhaps some may think that this is all theory and not fact. Many men are good and successful preachers with no knowledge of the ancient languages. The Methodists did a great work before they had colleges or an educated ministry. But the Methodists have always operated in a land of colleges. Their first generation of preachers were taught by the Wesleys, who were graduates of Oxford, the proudest of the English universities, and eminent Greek scholars; and many of these preachers, though without the advantages of early education, became most enthusiastic students of the original Scriptures, some of them committing large portions, and even the whole of the Greek Testament to memory, and all, in their extempore preaching able to expound the Hebrew text of any passage of the Old Testament which they had occasion to use. Many intensely interesting examples of this early Methodist scholarship are given by Southey in his biography of the Wesleys. They believed in their hearts that the original Scriptures were the word of God to men, and as the interpreters of God's word to the people they acted conscientiously in accordance with their belief. There is but one alternative—there must be either direct plenary inspiration, or a familiarity with the Bible in its original tongues, to qualify one to be an interpreter of God's word to the people. Such a scholarship as that of the first Methodists lasted a good while, and fertilized a wide field otherwise barren. But diffused through successive generations, and spreading over a large space, it began at last to run very thin. In this country especially, it fell off to a mere echo; and for the last thirty years the Methodists, with most commendable diligence, have been returning to the scholarship of their founders, and establishing everywhere in the land, literary institutions of a high order for both clergy and laity.

The Baptists, too, began their career among us, by decrying

human learning, and especially the study of the ancient languages; but the progress of society around them and their own good sense, have entirely changed both their opinions and their feeling in this respect; and now for zealous, earnest, persevering, successful study of the original languages of the Scriptures, there is no denomination whatever, which goes before the Baptists. And so it ever must be. Such is the mighty power of truth in the long run. Truth will force its way, sooner or later.

Uneducated men sometimes educate themselves and by their own supereminent talent become better trained than most of the educated; but these are rare examples, of men with great native powers, and are exceptions to the general rule. Such rare instances can not be calculated upon to supply the daily wants of the Church.

Uneducated men of only the average native power, in a limited sphere, and for special departments, are often eminently useful; but to give permanence and value to their work, they must be surrounded and sustained by the educated. They are like the rifle-rangers and light artillery, admirably effective in their peculiar line; but without the compact bodies, heavily armed, to form a base for their operations, easily scattered and worse than useless for any permanent achievement.

The revolver may say to the columbiad: "You great clumsy thing, you can not move without a team of twenty horses to start you, and you want an hour to turn round in; in a close fight, hand-to-hand, you can do nothing, and you cost heaps of money to begin with." "True, my lively little snapper," (replies the columbiad;) "but I can throw a three hundred pound iron ball five miles through the air, and at one blow sink a ship with a crew of a thousand men, while you are picking off some half-dozen enemies in detail with your leaden pellets." And this is just the difference between the erudite Calvin with his Institutes and the unlettered colporteur with his tracts. In the war with Satan and sin, we must have both, and both at the same time.

I have presented this subject—the indispensable necessity of colleges and literary institutions of the highest order, to the Church, for the accomplishment of its appropriate work—in only one of its aspects, the aspect in which it has most forcibly presented itself to my own mind, in consequence of the professional duties to which my life has been devoted. There are many other points of view no less important and impressive, and many of these have been presented with great ability and power in the reports of the Secretary of this Society and in the discourses of those who have before spoken at its anniversaries. Thank God, there is no difference of opinion among intelligent and earnest Christians as to the necessity of accomplishing the object contemplated by this Society. Here there is a wonderful, a most cheering unanimity. The only question is, whether this Society can not wait till some other objects have been accomplished first. If twenty years of most earnest and self-sacrificing labor on the ground give me any right to an opinion, I say, No, this Society can not wait a moment, its resources must all be put in requisition now, or the whole field to us is lost. General Knox always said that Washington lost the battle of Germantown, because he waited for a stone house to be demolished, before he would press on to meet the advancing foe. In this case his habitual caution and self-distrust operated disastrously. My health broke down in the West and I became entirely incapacitated for labor there, not from over-work, not from any thing which I actually had to do; but from constant anxiety lest the good Christians to whom God had committed the funds might be saying to themselves:

"Well, we will have our colporteurs and our missionaries and our meeting-houses first, and then after a while the people themselves will build their colleges." Dear brethren, there can be no first and last in this work. All must be first; your missionaries must be first, and your meeting-houses must be first, and your tracts must be first, and your colleges and theological schools must be first, and they must all be first, and they must all go together with one unbroken front or the whole battle is lost. All the divisions of the grand army must be moving on together, and there can be no waiting for any thing, any more than one leg can be waiting for the other, when a man is on a rapid march.

Happily this whole matter is now seen and appreciated in its true light. The labors of this Society have not been in vain. With the most gratifying liberality an enlightened Christian public is responding to its appeals, and our churches are true to the principles of their fathers in respect to the necessity of institutions of learning of the highest class, for the use of the Church in its fullest development.

As long as there are new States springing up West, and still west of us, until the whole country from the Atlantic Ocean to the Pacific is filled and cultivated and civilized and christianized, just so long must there be some method East for sustaining colleges West. Whatever may be our views of the mysteries of divine providence or on the nicer points of theological speculation, one thing is absolutely certain, and we are all agreed in it, namely, that we are put into this world to help each other, and whatever may be the origin of the evil in which the world is involved, there is but one way out of it, and that is by the word of God; and we can wield the power of the word of God by those methods only which the decree of divine providence has made effective, and which all Christian bodies, since the times of the Apostles, have been obliged to resort to.

And it is not brutish Australians, nor cannibal New-Zealanders, nor snake-eating Africans that we are laboring for, (though all these can be regenerated and brought to a life of purity and love by the Spirit and word of God, yet with a distressing seedtime and a long deferred harvest;) but we are extending a little temporary help (such as our fathers, in the infancy of their institutions, received from their beloved island home) to the noblest work of modern civilization, where the seedtime is all genial and lovely, and the harvest is almost simultaneous with it, as in some tropical orchards you may see the bud, the blossom, and the ripened fruit, all growing at the same time on the same tree. This is what we have seen, and still see, in our moral gardens at the West; and if we are faithful to the trust which God has put into our hands, we may continue to see it, till the whole space between the Atlantic and the Pacific is filled and exulting with a complete Christian civilization.

How nobly and efficiently the West comes forward in this hour of our country's need, in this last great struggle against barbarism and anarchy! And have the twenty years' labor of this Society had nothing to do with making the preparation for this great triumph of national principle over the meanest and most sectional selfishness? How many of the glorious men who are there leading this magnificent movement, think you, have been trained in the institutions which you have fostered, and which, without your aid, would have perished? Go on with your work—you can not afford to stop—scatter still more profusely your seed, the harvest comes at once, and the yield is a thousand fold.

But some may say: "It takes so long to get this thorough education, and the work is of such pressing and immediate urgency, that we must shorten the course by four or five years and have the men in the field sooner." But would it not be cheaper to contrive some way, or pray God to open some way, by which, for the present emergency, men might be born sixteen years old, and thus save all those long years which the body and mind at present need to acquire their compactness, consistency, and firmness? This would shorten the course, to be sure, in a way that would be worth the while; and shall we not get up education societies and prayer-meetings to effect a purpose so desirable? Every body sees the absurdity of this. We can never help God along in his work by the violation of his laws, whether physical or moral. God spurns all such help.

The Creator, by irrevocable laws, has fixed certain limits, has made certain periods of time indispensably necessary for the consolidating and the fitting for actual service, of the powers both of the body and mind, and it is all in vain for men to think of transgressing these limits, or essentially curtailing these periods of time, without injury. God will have his own way. He will not have men born with the strength and power and stature of sixteen years, however urgent the exigency may be; nor will he, in ordinary cases, have minds grow into the discipline necessary for good service in less time than the experience of ages has decided to be requisite for a truly liberal education. Uneducated preachers, who decry human learning and the study of languages, claim for themselves, as they must do to give any authority to their preaching, a special gift of the Spirit, an inward light, superseding to a great extent the necessity of the outward word. Indeed, among those who acknowledge the supernatural character of the Christian revelation, there are in fact but three theories possible (except in a few exceptional cases) of a worthy entrance into the Christian ministry, always admitting genuine piety to be in all cases the indispensable prerequisite, to wit:

1st. The external, authoritative, ecclesiastical impartation of ministerial gifts as held by the Papists and other High Churchmen; or

2d. A specific inspiration and infallible inward light, such as is claimed by many fanatical sects; or

3d. A knowledge of the Bible as God gave it to men at first by inspiration of the Holy Ghost, without the necessity of depending on uninspired translations.

We have deliberately and intelligently rejected the first two of these theories, and adopted the third. Now let us deliberately, intelligently, and consistently accept all the consequences of this principle, and act throughout in accordance with it.

www.ingramcontent.com/pod-product-compliance
Lightning Source LLC
LaVergne TN
LVHW011138110826
845150LV00008B/2393
* 9 7 8 1 4 1 8 1 9 3 5 0 8 *